In Grief

A MOTHER'S FIGHT TO CHOOSE JOY

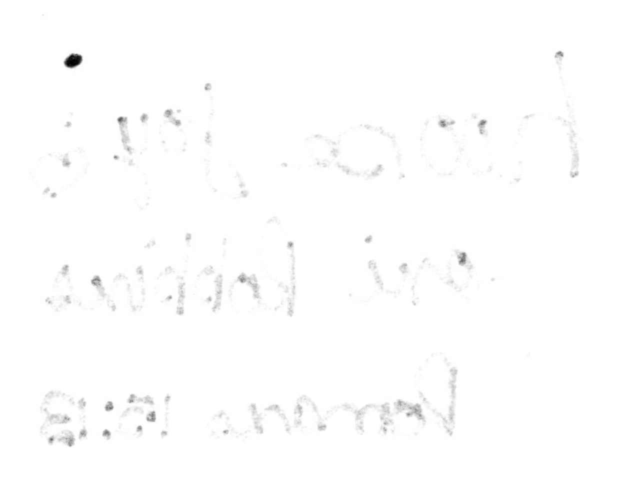

First Print Edition, 2024
Printed in China

Publishing Services: Jodi Cowles, Brandon Janous, and Rachael Mitchell (Blue Hat Publishing)
Cover Design: Rachael Mitchell (Blue Hat Publishing)
Interior Layout: Tim Marshall (Blue Hat Publishing)

ISBN (print): 978-1-962674-09-6
ISBN (ebook): 978-1-962674-22-5

BLUE HAT
PUBLISHING
BOISE • KNOXVILLE • NASHVILLE • SEATTLE
WWW.BLUEHATPUBLISHING.COM

Foreword

I clearly remember in May of 2021 when I received word that my dear friend Joni had lost her son through a terrible accident. Kay and I immediately fell lifeless as we prayed for her and her family. The Holy Spirit nudged me to call her phone, my knees somewhat weak waiting to see if she would take the call, rushing through my head was; what will I say, what can I say in such a time like this? How do you comfort a mother who lost her son to such a tragic event?

In my lifetime I have experienced losing close family members to death. My parents, my sisters, Kay's parents, many close friends, but there is no way to compare these deaths to what Joni had experienced. A mother's attachment to her children goes way beyond that of family members, the bond God gives a mother as she carries her child for nine months is such a miracle of God, it goes much deeper than one can ever imagine.

I knew from past experience from another close friend who lost a child that Joni could go one of two ways. She could blame God and become very resentful or she could feel His Grace and work through this hour by hour, minute by minute falling to His feet.

Joni Robbins chose the latter, during the pain few can realize she fell in the arms of Jesus and walked with Him through the valley of the shadow of death. Her husband by her side and surrounded by family and church family, she is walking to the other side of this tragedy.

As I relived her story, my heart once again felt her pain as she extracted previous thoughts to put on every page. As an author I can only imagine how she relived this May 17, 2021 event as she wrote each word.

I encourage every mother and every individual who has lost someone close to them not read this book but consume this book. Follow the heart of a lady and family that faced the ultimate test of faith.

God will use this book to lift up those who are having their faith challenged by losing a loved one. Joni exemplifies this passage when asking why?

"Praise be to the God and Father of our Lord Jesus Christ, the Father of compassion and God of all comfort, who comforts us in all our troubles, so that we can comfort those in any trouble with the comfort we ourselves received from God."

Joni, your Ethan will smile as you help thousands of mothers overcome the grief of losing a son.

Bob Goshen
Author of *Confident Hope*

To Anson, the reason I won't let myself drown.
I pray you continue to follow your dreams and trust
God's plan for your life, and Caitlyn's.

Always remember that even in the hard times,
He is still good.

Introduction

You know how all good stories begin with once upon a time? Well, once upon a time, our story was a kind of fairytale. After meeting on a blind date, Chad and I fell hard and fast and have been married for twenty-five years. Over those years, we had experienced life's ups and downs, including several miscarriages, but we were finally basking in the joy of raising two wonderful sons, Anson and Ethan.

We lived in a small and friendly town in eastern North Carolina where we knew the names of all our neighbors and couldn't take a quick trip to the grocery store or post office without running into friends. As entrepreneurs, we were able to set our own schedules and spend a lot of quality time with our boys when they were growing up. Our small businesses were thriving, we'd purchased our dream home, and we lived at the center of a robust community of family and friends with whom we regularly gathered to worship Jesus and try to grow in our faith.

It wasn't all easy, but the season we were moving through was incredibly sweet. Chad, our boys, and me were living our own little version of happily ever after.

But on May 17th, 2021, our lives tragically changed.

This is the story of a fairytale gone wrong, of a happily ever after blown all apart, and of a God big enough to stand with us in the rubble as we began to rebuild.

PART 1

FC
IN MEMORY OF
Ethan
ROBBINS

CHAPTER ONE

May 17, 2021

Nice to meet you, I'm Joni Robbins. And I'm about to take you on a journey with me. One of grief, but also–if you can believe me–of joy. I will have to ask you to hang in there with me because it's imperative to start at the beginning.

Ironically, it was a gorgeous day. The flowers were starting to bloom, and Chad's beloved zoysia grass was luscious and green. The pool had recently been opened, and the boys had taken a dip or two thanks to some unseasonably warm temperatures in our area. The details of the morning are crystal clear in my memory.

Because of the challenges of remote learning during Covid, my youngest son, Ethan, had been struggling to pass algebra. It was near the end of the school year, so it was crunch time. A friend of his had helped him study for an exam over the weekend and because I thought the exam was that day, I woke early to make him a full breakfast.

"Hey bud, would you rather have sausage or bacon with your breakfast?" I yelled up to him from the bottom floor, leaning on the banister and, while I waited for his answer, taking a sip of the healthy green tea energy drinks I favored at the time.

"I'm fine," his voice drifted down.

"I wanted to make you a nice breakfast before your exam." You mothers might be able to recognize the tone of voice I used.

"Oh," he answered, "Today is just a review day."

"Oh!" I echoed, surprised. I guess I could have slept in anyway. "I thought today was the exam day," I mumbled, showing that my caffeine had not quite kicked in yet.

"Nope, not today," he said as he leaned over the balcony with a smile on his face, "But I'll take sausage."

"You want some milk with that?" as I shuffled to the kitchen, taking another big, caffeinated sip.

"Nah. I'll just have water."

I poured some ice water into a fancy glass water goblet and kept an eye on the sizzling sausage while I made toast with butter and strawberry jelly. I scrambled the eggs and made sure the sausage was nice and crispy like he liked it. A couple of wrens and a cardinal were circling the feeder outside the open kitchen window, adding their voices to the music I had playing quietly. I'm not going to pretend we were living in a Hallmark movie, but that morning was pretty close.

When Ethan came down, I served everything up with a pretty napkin and a nice plate right next to the beautiful flowers left over from a baby shower I had hosted over the weekend.

I'll never forget standing beside him at the kitchen island, watching him eat. He loved good food, and I knew he enjoyed every bite. I don't remember if I told him I loved him or to drive safely when he left for school, but I probably did. I usually did.

That was the last time I saw him alive.

It was a very busy day. Chad and I worked together on real estate appointments, and when we were done, we went to our favorite Italian restaurant for a late lunch. I texted Ethan and asked if he wanted anything to eat. He was studying at home with the same friend he had studied with over the weekend. He texted me back, saying to bring home a large cheese pizza. I asked him if his friend was a vegetarian, and he replied, "No, Mom, she isn't gonna eat."

It wasn't until I got home that I realized there were four girls with him. Ethan had three friends there, all sisters, plus the girl who was helping him study. I heard them laughing and carrying on upstairs in the bonus room. While I went into the family room and plopped down on a comfy couch to get in a little reading, Chad took the pizza up to them and asked them how the studying was going.

It was the last time he'd see Ethan alive.

At around 7p.m. I was still sitting in the family room after a phone call, happy to hear Ethan and his friends playing pool above me. The pool cue crashing into all the balls is a distinct sound. I considered going upstairs and breaking up the party–after all, the girls were here to help him study, not play around. But they were laughing and having such a good time. After the loneliness and isolation of Covid, I knew they were all longing to be with friends, so I stayed downstairs and just let them have fun.

A few minutes later, I heard a loud noise. I thought that just couldn't have been what it sounded like, there is no way. Absolutely no way. For one long moment, I decided if I didn't move it wouldn't be real. It couldn't be real. But Levi and Elsie, our Australian Shepherds, were barking, and the girls were screaming, so I pulled myself from the couch and headed up the stairs.

At the top of the stairs I met a wildly frantic girl, an expression on her face I will never forget. "Ethan was playing around, and he accidentally shot himself, and I have to get out of here!" I entered the room and saw him on the ground, eyes and mouth wide open with no apparent signs of life.

In shock at what I was seeing, I threw my phone and then immediately and frantically started looking for it to call 911. I found one of the girls' phones right next to me but couldn't figure out how to make it work, so I just started praying.

As I prayed, I held my hand over the gunshot wound to the right side of his head; it was at the very back. I truly believed maybe it only skimmed the back of his head and he would be okay. I envisioned prayer warriors praying so hard that God would change His mind and let my baby boy–seventeen, but still very much my baby–live and not die. Maybe there would be a miracle and people all over the world would hear about it and come to Christ because of it. I prayed and prayed, envisioning a long road of recovery with many miracles along the way, but that isn't what we got.

Time stood still as I prayed, but eventually, it started speeding back up. I began to notice that nothing seemed to be happening and no one had come to help, so I made the decision to prop Ethan's pillow up behind his head and run downstairs and outside to scream for help.

Chad and our neighbor were across the street, so when they heard me yell, they came running. I don't know what I screamed other than help, but Chad immediately and calmly called 911 before we all ran back up the stairs and I went back to Ethan's side. I don't remember doing this, but Chad says I suddenly came back into the room and prayed like I was at a revival. I begged God in shouts and screams to raise Ethan up like he had raised Lazurus.

But He did not.

After what felt like forever, a young guy in an EMT uniform arrived. We were so relieved to see him come up the stairs. I don't know how long he worked on Ethan. Chad and I were sitting and watching out of his way so he could do his job. It seemed only a few moments went by before he turned to us and said, "He's gone."

This did not compute in my brain, and I responded, "Aren't you even gonna work on him? Can't you take him to the hospital?" He answered, "Ma'am, you don't want him like this."

Those words–though delivered in a compassionate and professional tone–pierced my soul, and somehow, I understood what he was really saying. If we managed to get Ethan on life support, it would only be for long enough to say goodbye; then we'd have to pull the plug. Would that path be any easier? At least we could formally say goodbye, but then again, I don't think "easy" exists in this scenario.

A second EMT materialized out of nowhere. I hadn't even seen him enter, but he came up to me and said, "Ma'am, let's go get you cleaned up." As he gently led me from the room, I looked down to see my hands and arms were covered with Ethan's blood. I am a feisty person, but I didn't even argue with him. I followed him out, washed up, and they never let me go back upstairs.

Soon after, our house was full of neighbors and friends. Our pastors came, all of them. Chad's parents and sister arrived, and our home became a revolving door of friends and family, bringing tears, food, and physical expressions of care. There were cars lined up all the way down the road.

Anson walked over from his apartment, over the detached garage, deeply distraught but very concerned about me and Chad. We were all in disbelief about what just happened. The father of Caitlyn, his girlfriend at the time, drove her here to comfort Anson.

I will never forget my cousins showing up almost immediately. One of them was a state trooper who heard about the accident over the radio and called his siblings. They had all been here for the baby shower the Saturday before. The youngest refused to leave us that night and stayed in his truck to make sure we were all safe.

One of our friends who was battling cancer read on Facebook about Ethan's passing in the middle of the night and drove straight to our house to pray for us. My sweet cousin was there to greet him. I am so glad those two got to meet when they did because our friend lost his battle with cancer about ten months later.

The days following the accident are a blur. Crying. Lack of sleep. Stomach pain. It's a fog that only lifts in snapshots. The time someone forced me to eat, and I ended up choking on the food. Friends and family members talked us out of staying in our home that night, so we all crammed in Anson's apartment and attempted to sleep on an air mattress. We had extremely hard conversations with well-meaning organizations wanting us to donate body parts. Our pastors were speaking to us on the side porch. I can't remember a thing they said, but I do remember everyone not wanting us to go back inside and how uncomfortable that wooden bench was.

My body was alive, but my soul, my brain, and my heart felt dead. I didn't know how I was supposed to keep living, leaving my child behind.

Two days later, on Wednesday, we had to go to the funeral home. As I was trying to put myself together, I noticed I still had Ethan's blood caked around my fingernails and I didn't want to wash it off. That's also the first time I noticed I had bruises on my arms and legs from where I had held onto Ethan.

I remember the Holy Spirit whispering to me, comforting me as I washed the last of his blood off.

At the funeral home, we picked out Ethan's casket. A casket. For my son. We gave them the clothes and shoes we chose for him to be buried in. The director asked if I would like them to cut a small lock of his hair. I smiled weakly, thinking about his silky, shoulder-length, dark-blonde hair. I did. I knew I needed a lock of his hair and had brought my scissors with me. By the time he asked, I already had Ethan's hair in my purse from when we were alone in the room with him. But I didn't tell them that, so they just cut off some more.

I will never forget a friend showing up to pray with me over Ethan's body. I don't know that I was able to breathe, much less pray, but she prayed so boldly, and I will never forget it.

They asked me for Ethan's Social Security card, and as I slid it over to the funeral director, the Holy Spirit gently spoke to me again, "Look at the numbers, 052817. The 28 is for the day Ethan was born, the 28th day of January. The 05 and 17 are for the day he would go home—May 17th. I told you, you couldn't have stopped this. May 17th, 2021 was just his day."

Though it didn't fix anything or take my deep grief away, seeing the corresponding numbers and hearing from the Holy Spirit gave me a small assurance, knowing that even this most horrific circumstance was filtered through God's hand.

CHAPTER TWO

Ethan Patrick Robbins

When Ethan was five years old, we were sitting side by side during a Christmas program in the church gym, where we held events that the sanctuary was too small for. It was a wonderful program and all that was left was the traditional altar call every good pastor likes to give in case the program had moved someone to give their life to Christ.

I admit I took it all a little bit for granted. I was thinking of something I'd forgotten to pick up for lunch. Can you believe I can't even remember what the item was now? What I do remember is that I was already gathering my purse and phone and planning a hasty exit when Ethan tugged on my arm and looked up at me and Chad with sparkling blue eyes.

"God told me to go up there," and up he marched.

Ethan was a fairly shy child, and in that particular season, he was sticking pretty close to my side. But that morning, he walked up to that altar to meet Jesus, and he never looked back.

I remember people saying that he was so young; did he really know what he was doing? I believe he did. I don't remember any other kids or adults going up before him to make him feel like he should, too. God told him to go, and Ethan was obedient.

He was baptized the following March after meeting with our pastor, who said, "He may only be five, but in reality, he understands about as much as the average adult does when they first meet Jesus."

But he was also a typical boy. When he was six years old, he nearly set the woods behind our friend's home on fire by trying to cook a hot dog. Ethan and our friend's son took one piece of charcoal, a child-proof lighter, and, of course, one hot dog to the woods to cook. They happened to be right on highly flammable dry pine straw.

We were in front of the house because we had a local photographer come and take photos for us in the car we had just earned in our direct sales company. Anson hadn't wanted to play that evening, so he was crouching down in the back seat so he wouldn't be seen. Then, our friend's daughter came running around the corner to announce that her brother and Ethan had caught the woods on fire and were trying to put it out with styrofoam cups and water from the garden hose. Thankfully, our friend used to be a firefighter and got it all under control.

When he was about nine, Ethan chopped down a tree with a machete. He was a very compliant child and had asked for permission first. I am pretty sure we had just finished learning about George Washington cutting down a cherry tree in homeschool and he was inspired to cut a tree down himself.

We asked him why he wanted to use a machete and he said something along the lines of "every real man needs to chop a tree down with a machete." When he was done, we asked him what he thought and he said, "I think I have blisters and don't need to ever do that again!"

We are so thankful to have been able to spend lots of time with our boys during the five years we homeschooled. We have some of the fondest memories of traveling together, but one of my most favorites was a trip to Maine with just me and Ethan.

At that point he had never flown, but he'd heard Chad and I speak about the full-sized drinks and snacks that JetBlue passed out. We flew JetBlue to Logan in Boston, and I let my seven year old pick out our rental car. Of course, he picked a red convertible Camaro. We drove up to Maine where he accompanied me to several home parties for my direct sales business.

One of those homes just happened to have a chicken coop outside, and for whatever reason, Ethan and the other kids there played in it. Little did I know he had feathers all over his shoes. Well, until I saw them as he climbed into the car. Needless to say, I am sure whoever cleaned that car after returning it found lots of feathers. We tried rolling down all of the windows and letting them blow out, but it just didn't work. It was peak leaf season and the drive back to Boston was stunning, feathers and all.

Our last trip, just the two of us, was equally as special. He went with me to Tennessee in March of 2019. He had just gotten his driver's permit and I let him drive the entire way there and back. He navigated us through the mountains with heavy rain and fog. I felt so safe with him behind the wheel because he was such a good driver. And he also had the best road trip playlist as well.

Ethan was good and kind and soft-spoken. He always had a shoulder ready for someone to cry on and an ear to listen when his friends needed him most. He was the biggest helper and wise beyond his years; he would listen well and then give great advice. He could be trusted to take care of things and help out anytime anyone needed him. When he had dances at school he always had me get a red rose for his date, saying, "Every pretty girl deserves a beautiful red rose."

In tenth grade 2020, Ethan's Bible teacher asked the students to pick a life verse. Ethan chose Romans 15:13, "May the God of Hope fill you with all JOY and peace as you trust in Him, so that you may overflow with Hope by the power of the Holy Spirit."

How could this tragic event have taken place in our home? I suppose in the same way many tragic events happen–through the collision of minor, unimportant events with small, unfortunate mishaps. One insignificant link after another, until the chain of grief is inevitably formed and laid around your heart.

I was never a fan of guns, but hunting was a way of life for Chad growing up, and he passed that love on to Ethan. Ethan wanted a gun for many years and Chad bought him one for his fifteenth birthday. It was locked securely away in our gun safe, Chad the only one with access. But on Black Friday, about seven months before the accident, a local store had gun safes on sale and Chad bought a bigger one to house his growing collection. He and Ethan put the safe in a different location than the smaller one which happened to be quite far from our bedrooms.

Ethan thought it was crazy and irresponsible that if there were an intruder we wouldn't be able to get to our guns. He asked Chad if he could put his new twenty-two in his room, in two separate pieces and in two different places. That way, if someone were to find one piece, they wouldn't be likely to find the other. Chad would be the only one to know where the magazine was, and he hid it well.

I remember telling Chad, "You know, I don't like guns; they are not my thing. You will have to make that decision." I never thought twice about it again and trusted Chad's wisdom and guidance for Ethan.

Ethan wasn't just interested in guns and hunting; he had also wanted to be a law enforcement officer since he was old enough to speak. When he was young and people asked him what he wanted to be when he grew up, without hesitation, he replied, "a pleace."

That strong desire continued into his teenage years, and he was so excited when he was invited to a junior law enforcement leadership event in Washington DC. Not only for his own goals but also because Chad had done something similar when he was in high school. We were all excited for him, but because of Covid, the event was canceled. Ethan was so disappointed.

A year prior to the accident, when Ethan had completed his driving test to receive his driver's license, the instructor told me how good of a driver he was and that he had excellent hand-eye coordination. He mentioned Ethan would be great in some sort of law enforcement because of his rare ability to back up through traffic cones. The instructor had only seen a few complete the task without knocking over a cone–Ethan did it with ease.

Ethan looked at me and said, "See Mom, I was just born to be in law enforcement." That was when I knew I was going to have to be okay with his dream of being a law enforcement officer. It wasn't easy–I'll admit, I had a mother's worries that he would realize his dream and be in danger every single day. But I realized at that moment that I needed to set those worries aside and stop trying to convince him to "keep his options open." I decided to trust him and his future to God, who I knew was powerful enough to protect him in any job.

Ethan was always tall for his age, bigger than most of his classmates, and very mature and trustworthy. But he was also a seventeen-year-old boy who thought he was invincible. "His day" was a perfect storm of wanting to prove to his friends guns are safe and being a typical, not-always-wise, seventeen-year-old boy.

I will never know this side of heaven why he felt the need to show his friends that gun, even though the magazine was NOT in the gun. Why? And why there was a single bullet in the chamber, or why he let his finger get anywhere near that trigger–but he did.

He knew how to handle guns safely and responsibly. He knew the basic gun rule that "there could always be one in the chamber," but that day he felt literally bulletproof.

CHAPTER THREE
A Dream of Peace

In the early morning hours of May 22nd, 2021, I had a dream. I had been awake all night anticipating the visitation later that day. Finally, around 4 a.m. I was praying–or really just begging God to get me through the day–because that was what my prayer life was like at that point. Finally, my eyes began to close, and I drifted off to sleep.

I woke to the most beautiful scenery. I could see fields of uncut grass that sparkled and shined with bright greens and yellows. There were absolutely no shadows anywhere. For months after the dream, I remember staring at the leaves on any trees I would pass by, wondering how the leaves in my dream could have been so perfect. Every leaf casts a shadow here, but not in my dream.

After I had taken in the gorgeous scenery and been able to breathe without gasping for air for the first time since the accident, I saw someone approaching me. Or maybe I should say something? She, I guess, had on a long linen, very simple, almost sackcloth dress with a simple, thin, beige rope for a belt. I couldn't see her feet, or maybe I just didn't notice them because her hair was astonishing.

Her hair was like liquified silver, not when it is so hot that it glows orange, but just as it is beginning to cool down. I remember wanting to touch it but feeling like maybe I shouldn't. Not because it might be hot, but because that would just be awkward. Since I was a hairdresser for so long, I still pay quite a bit of attention to hair, and hers was absolutely stunning.

Now let me tell you about her face. Ok, so her face. It looked like a light bulb, but it was the softest white light. You could stare at it, and it wouldn't hurt your eyes at all. There were no facial features. It was just light.

The sky was light. Like a light bulb, but again, it didn't hurt your eyes to stare up at it. It wasn't blue, so it just didn't look like the sky at all—no clouds, no sun, just light.

This lady/angel was going to be my guide through whatever I was getting ready to experience, and of course, I had questions. So many questions. But I wasn't scared at all. I could tell she was leading me to a small simple park bench. I couldn't wait to ask her a question and I quickly said, "I just need to know why?"

She quickly responded back, and actually, neither of us had to use words; we just knew what the other was thinking, which was a really good thing for her since she didn't have ears or a mouth. Her response gave me so much peace. She simply said, "I can't tell you that until you are here yourself."

I know this was a dream, but it felt so real. I felt like I had been taken to the outskirts of heaven. I will be so happy to be there and thank Jesus for His sacrifice and then grab my Ethan and tell him how much I love him. All of the questions we have will be gone because we will be together forever and none of it will matter anymore.

She led me over to a park bench which had wood rails and wrought-iron armrests and feet. I sat to her left. I remember taking in my surroundings and I finally said, "I'm worried that Ethan is lonely. He doesn't know anyone who has passed away."

I looked to my left, and it was like a TV screen popped up into the air–there were these gorgeous trees behind it. I saw Ethan as a little boy, maybe six or eight. He was in a field playing with seven or eight children. I couldn't see anything about them. It was like this was blocked from me. I could really only see their silhouettes. I had this feeling that he somehow knew these children.

And when I was there or in this dream, we didn't have to move lips, you just had a thought and it was responded to. The thought popped up in my mind that maybe these were the children we had miscarried and then immediately I knew I was correct. Oh, what I have to look forward to in heaven one day! I will finally have the big family I always wanted! I got the feeling that he had somehow known these children all along.

Next, I asked, "Why this way?" The screen to my left popped up again and I saw four of these light-faced people/angels sitting around a round table, my guide being one of them. The one to her right said, "Well, this is easy, he has a car. Teenagers die in car wrecks all of the time." My guide said, "No, we can't do that. The mom has prayed fervently over all of their vehicles. This would cause her to lose her faith." As I heard their voices, I could see Ethan on the road right outside of our neighborhood, his white Tahoe spinning out of control and his face scraping across the asphalt. Then we ran to him, and we were trying to resuscitate him. I am sure that he was already gone while we were working on him.

The next one said, "They have a pool." Again, I could see this play out like a scene in a movie. Our pool is barely five feet deep at one point and it is not a pool for diving. I watched him dive in and then myself trying to pull his lifeless body from the pool. My person said, "No, the mom will have to walk past that pool every day and she will never get back in it."

The next one said, "There is a gun in his room." My person said, "Would it be instant?" The other one said, "It could be." And then my person said the strangest thing, "Ok, I guess that is the most humane way."

That was the end of the dream. Believe it or not, God has always spoken to me through my dreams, and I can't explain the amount of peace this one provided and continues to provide.

It makes me feel like May 17th, 2021, was just the day Ethan would go to his eternal home and there was nothing I or anyone would have been able to do to stop it. I would do anything to have him back, but the raw truth is, that cannot happen. What can happen is that I can learn to live without the guilt and shame of his death and know that for whatever reason, God saw fit for Ethan to go home that day.

CHAPTER FOUR

The Days I Wish Didn't Exist

That first week, I had to tell myself the truth multiple times a day just to be able to get out of bed. I hadn't fixed my hair or worn makeup since the day of the accident. I didn't know how I was ever going to be able to stop crying long enough to wear makeup or have the strength to fix my hair and put on clothes. I decided shorts and T-shirts would just be my new uniform for a while.

Our community surrounded and bolstered us. One of the youth from church came over and straightened up our house because–even though I couldn't do it myself–it mattered to me. The church brought over a huge spaghetti feast. One of Ethan's friends and her mother went shopping to get me a pair of black shoes for the funeral. We had a Meal Train that lasted for 60 days.

As we were preparing for the visitation, a dear friend mentioned she'd never seen Ethan without a hat. She was right–he was never without a hat–but I couldn't imagine having him wear a baseball cap. She asked if she could help. Ethan had worn a big, white cowboy hat to prom, and she didn't want us to have to use that one, so she bought an identical hat and cut off the back half. It was just perfect.

The week was filled with decisions I never wanted to make and grief I never thought I'd have to bear. On Wednesday, Thursday, and Friday Ethan lay in repose. We went on that Wednesday, and it was one of the hardest days of our lives.

On Saturday evening, we had a visitation at the church where the boys went to preschool because our church just wasn't large enough. It was a chance for people to come and share their condolences with our family and it was hard. I hadn't even begun to process my son's death myself and it was hard to synthesize everyone else's grief as well. It was all too much.

That being said, I am grateful we did the visitation. It was an important part of the grief process and, though everyone was a mess, we were all a mess together grieving the loss of a wonderful young man gone way too soon.

The day after the visitation was Sunday, the day of the funeral. I was glad I had the chance to speak with so many people the day before. It was a beautiful service. I have been on the Praise and Worship team at our church for years, and some of our team came and played.

Ethan's guitar and Bible teacher sang "Good Good Father." Ethan was in his 8th-grade guitar class, and he already knew how to play some and could help the other kids too. His teacher gave him the "Good Good Father" award on awards day. It was kind of a running joke because they played it so many times to help the other kids learn.

In addition to our current pastors, the pastor who baptized Ethan eleven years prior came and spoke. That was so special to us, and I will never be able to adequately thank him.

Four of Ethan's friends bravely spoke at his funeral. I am not sure how they were able to, but they did, and I will never forget the kind words they shared.

I don't know why I had thought about it before, but I'd always said that if I lost a child. I wouldn't go to the funeral–I would be in my closet screaming. But now that it had happened to me, I knew I had to go. I remember telling God that He would have to get me through it, and He did. He gave me the peace that passes all understanding. I knew at the time that it was temporary, that the peace put on us would not last forever, but I had it during the funeral. I sang, I praised, I worshiped God–at the top of my lungs and with all of my heart.

It was such a beautiful service and there were people who accepted Christ that day, but there were some awkward parts too. After the service they walked us out through the center aisle, in front of probably 1,000 people, and I remember asking myself, "Am I supposed to look at my feet?" I'm normally such a friendly person, greeting everyone, and I didn't know where to look. I remember seeing a friend and waving but then thinking that my action was inappropriate.

After the funeral was one of the moments I was dreading the most: the burial. Though I knew in my head and my heart that Ethan's spirit was immediately present with Jesus in heaven a moment after the accident, I had a hard time with the physical aspect of Ethan's body still on earth. As his mother, it wasn't "just" his body, but it was the body I prayed and believed for, grew inside my own for nine months, and loved and cared for, for 17 years. I was connected to that body, and I did not want that casket to drop into that ground.

Tragedy and comedy are two threads from the same tapestry, and there was a bit of comedy woven into one of our most tragic days just before the visitation. Chad's cousin, the one who introduced us, called us in a panic as we were scrambling to get ready and out the door. I felt like I was moving in slow motion and just couldn't function even though I knew I had to. I remember my phone ringing and then Chad's. We both ignored it because we just didn't have time to chat.

Let's face it, we ignored most calls at that point. Finally, I answered my phone figuring it must be important.

"Joni! Bentley fell in the hole!"

"What? What hole?"

"Ethan's grave!"

"I came to pay respects at my mama's grave and brought Bentley. He ran over to Ethan's spot and tried to jump over the plywood covering the hole but didn't quite make it and he fell in the hole!"

It took me a minute to even process what she was telling me. Her one-eyed dog, Bentley, fell into the six-foot-deep hole prepared for Ethan's casket. How was that possible? Why did he try to jump over it? Why'd she bring him? Did the dog break any bones falling down that far?

"Well, is he still in there?"

"Yeah! Can you ask Chad to come down here and help me get him out?"

I was too stunned to laugh, or weep, or even get mad. It was what it was. Her dog fell in the hole, didn't break any legs, and the fire department had to come retrieve the dog. She has pictures to prove it. Chad couldn't go help because we were already almost late for our son's visitation. It was a very unusual situation, one that we laughed at later.

The Grave Truth

I want to explain how I feel about going to Ethan's grave site. Some people, really most people, find comfort in going to "visit" their loved one's grave site, and there is a lot of societal pressure that I should be doing that regularly.

But that's not me. I absolutely do not like going. The things I think about when I am there are not good. I don't even like to ride by the cemetery. And for the longest time, I wouldn't go past it. This meant I had to take the long way home and I didn't care. Chad would always go right by the cemetery, and I just didn't understand why. How could he drive right past the land where our son is buried? I even went as far as to turn my head so I wouldn't even have to see it.

I think about silly things like, is he cold? Of course, he isn't cold, he isn't there. He is in heaven with Jesus and having so much fun that he wouldn't come back if he could! And then I think, if he isn't here, then why am I here? My mind can really go to bad places fast, like, what does he look like now? Did his body move a lot when they closed the casket? But if he isn't really there, but wait, the remains of his earthly body are there. We didn't put his shoes on his feet, should we have? My mind just goes to the craziest places, and it is pretty hard to be okay for a while after a trip to the graveyard.

I don't know how to explain any better than this–think of a beloved heirloom, passed down through your family. Something like your grandma's rocking chair. You love it. You cherish it. You expect to rock your grandchildren in it. And then one day, totally unexpectedly, you have to put it in a hole.

I grew that body inside my own. I held it. I kissed its scraped knees. And though I know his spirit is in a better place, putting that body in a hole hurt.

Almost every time I have gone to his grave, I have heard the Holy Spirit tell me he isn't there and if going there makes me feel awful, just don't go. So, I simply don't go very often. Our sweet friend who owns a florist makes sure he has seasonally appropriate flowers throughout the year because it is a task I just can't complete.

dancing
Heaven

PART 2

In Grief, Be Present

I went where I was told to go that first week, put on clothes appropriate to the event, and automatically spoke the words that were expected. I was present physically, but at war with it all internally. It felt like I'd left my brain somewhere behind, still struggling to reckon with the bleak reality that my baby was gone.

For weeks that turned into months, I didn't want to leave our house. Chad went to the grocery store for me most of the time because it seemed like I'd melt down each time I tried. I remember taking our niece out for lunch and completely losing it in the restaurant when a song by one of Ethan's favorite country artists came on. If I had to go somewhere, I'd make Chad go with me. For some reason, if we were together people wouldn't ask, but if someone caught me alone, they'd go right for it.

Many wondered if I'd be able to walk upstairs again, but that wasn't as difficult. The first thing we did after the funeral was to restore the room Ethan passed away in. It was really a bonus room and guest space but the boys had each chosen to make it their "room" as they got older. A company was hired to come in and clean up everything. Friends and family members took care of every detail. They even hired painters and had the carpet replaced. And very quickly, it became a family room again, a place to remember, and a space of peace…

But as you can imagine, it was not so easy to clean up the wreckage of my inner life. My body, my soul, my marriage, my faith, even something as intrinsic as my personality–none of these things would ever be the same.

CHAPTER FIVE

Weep

I was sitting at the kitchen table a few days after the accident. Chad was in the garage with a couple of buddies. I'm not sure where Anson was. A good friend who had volunteered to help me with the slide show for the funeral had come over. I thought I could choose the photos, but I was hit by another wave of grief and just couldn't. Thankfully she took charge and got it done for us.

My body folded in on itself, and though I was vaguely aware of my friend's hand on my shoulder, it felt like my mind and spirit were on another plane. She passed me a tissue and I wiped automatically, but then came back to myself when I saw that the tissue was dry.

I was hunched and heaving, making the sounds that go along with weeping, but there were no tears coming from my eyes. My mind felt like it was wading through concrete trying to make connections, until I finally held the dry tissue up to my friend and shrugged my shoulders at her like, look, now I'm going crazy!

"Did you know that the body stops producing tears at a certain point?" she said. "It's to prevent dehydration–your body is trying to help you survive." And she scooted her chair even closer and held me in a tight hug. "Don't worry, you'll cry again."

Some people think that deep grief is a sign of weakness. To be honest–and not to my credit–I used to think that our relationship with our risen Savior, Jesus, should be able to keep us from deep grief. Until I lost Ethan.

In his letter to the Thessalonian church, Paul addresses grief when talking about the day of the Lord's coming, *"But I do not want you to be ignorant, brethren, concerning those who have fallen asleep, lest you sorrow as others who have no hope. For if we believe that Jesus died and rose again, even so, God will bring with Him those who sleep in Jesus." 1 Thessalonians 4:13-14 NKJV*

Paul meant that my grief would be different than someone who isn't in relationship with Christ because those in Christ have the promise of seeing their loved ones again in heaven. I thought, because of Jesus we wouldn't grieve as hard. I was wrong. But Paul wanted the early Christians to be informed so that they would grieve differently than the world grieves. Paul didn't condemn grief. In fact, he knew we would grieve.

The Apostle Paul knew sadness was a regular part of life, and he shared hopeful words with the people who followed Jesus. He wanted them to experience a different kind of sadness, one that recognizes the hope found in Christ. I couldn't shake the pain after losing Ethan, but I realized that because grief exists in scripture, I didn't put pressure on myself with unrealistic expectations to not cry or grieve.

Crying is not a sign of weakness. Jesus cried too, so I knew I was in good company. The shortest verse in the Bible, John 11:35, "Jesus wept" gives us permission to weep because Jesus wept at the grave of Lazarus. Jesus wept even though He knew He was about to raise Lazarus from the dead! He knew the future but still wept. He knew the joy that was coming, yet still, he wept.

I like to think He was weeping for the friends and family of Lazarus who didn't know what Jesus was about to do. I like to believe that He could feel their pain. So following Jesus' example, I stopped feeling guilty for my emotions. I gave myself the space to feel and know that it was alright–biblical even–to grieve. It's part of being human, and it's part of the journey toward healing. I knew enough to know not giving myself time to grieve wasn't good at all and without embracing the grief and tears it would surface again.

If you know me well, you know that I love hydrangeas. I love mopheads, and panicles, and all of the gorgeous colors! That's probably why we had so many hydrangeas at the funeral.

I gave away a lot of them, but I tried to keep one of each kind. That meant seven new hydrangeas to plant, and I knew exactly where I wanted them. We planted them right by the dock where Ethan had spent so much time fishing. Chad assured me there were sprinklers to keep them watered. If you know anything about hydrangeas, you know that they absolutely need to stay hydrated.

Sometime in July I fertilized those seven hydrangeas, just like I did all of my others, and when you fertilize, you must keep them really hydrated or the fertilizer will literally burn them up and they will die.

I remember that night like it was last night. I was on the phone with my best friend, "Hey, how are you?"

"Yeah, I'm out here in the yard admiring all my flowers. It was a nice day today, but dang, it was hot."

"What'd you do today?" It was almost dark, nearing 9 p.m. as I wandered through our amazing backyard. It was probably still about 85 degrees out and humid after reaching about 100 that afternoon. I made my way down toward the dock to check on my funeral hydrangeas.

"Oh!!" I inhaled sharply and interrupted my friend in the middle of her story. As I closed the gate behind me, I was mortified.

"What?" She panicked, always on alert around me.

"My funeral hydrangeas!" I wailed.

"What? What's wrong with them? What happened?" She knew how much I loved them and specifically why those specific bushes were so important to me.

"All of them are dead!" I screeched.

"The hydrangeas?" She clarified, probably triggered by other conversations we had.

"Yes! Oh my gosh!" The first plant was withered with no signs of life. I went to each one, carrying my friend on the phone with me, and pulled back the pine straw,

"They're ALLLLL dead." I burst into tears and cried hysterically.

"Joni, Joni! Are you ok? Do you need me to come over?"

"No!! This is Chad's fault! He killed them! He promised the sprinklers would reach! I can't believe he didn't notice he was killllling my funeral hydrangeas!!"

The death of the hydrangeas put me into a downward spiral, beating myself up about not being able to keep things alive. Blaming myself was a real feeling I would have a lot after Ethan passed away. Even though these emotions were over silly funeral plants, unpredictable events created unpredictable emotions.

I was so unkind to Chad over the funeral hydrangeas. As a fixer, he offered to get more and rearrange the sprinklers to do a better job of keeping them watered. At that point I didn't want my flowers fixed; I just wanted my broken heart fixed.

Later, I discovered that the funeral hydrangeas were florist hydrangeas and rarely ever make it if planted in the yard. I felt terrible for the way I treated Chad since I blamed the whole thing on him. I was very irrational and now I know that being irrational over the littlest things is normal when you've suffered a significant loss.

The amount of weeping that goes on after the loss of a child is incomprehensible and I did a whole lot of it for a very long time.

I also did a lot of ice cream eating. My helper in this was my best friend's daughter–almost my daughter too, although I didn't get to write her off on our taxes or have to pay her college tuition! I could send her a message and say something as simple as "I need ice cream." Or maybe, "I have ice cream, let's eat it!" She would know that meant I needed a cry session over a bowl of whatever we had or the local dollar store had. Sometimes we didn't even bother with a bowl, just two spoons and a container of ice cream. I always felt better after a good long cry and a bowl of ice cream.

Almost every day when Anson got home from work he would come and just sit on the couch, that very same couch where I heard that loud thud on May 17th. I would lay my weary head on Anson's strong shoulder and just weep. We really didn't say much but those were the most precious of times between a mother and a son.

For whatever reason, I could let it all out to Anson but not Chad. Why was this? If I have to guess I really think it has a lot to do with hurting Chad. I feel like if we could just try not to cry in front of each other we won't be as miserable. If he cried, I would cry, and if I cried he would cry. I guess I was trying to be strong for him and him for me.

CHAPTER SIX

Struggle

I have asked, "Why?" a million times over. Why was this God's plan? Why was it Ethan's day? Why did it have to be like this? I had long, drawn-out conversations with God, asking Him, why?

Why did this happen to our family? I always felt God took care of us and Ethan's death felt far, far outside of that secure feeling.

Why did this happen to me? Honestly, hadn't I suffered enough? Me, who was rejected by my biological parents. Me, who spent three of my first four years in a hospital. Me, who lost my grandfather at age nine and my grandmother at age twenty-two–the only "parents" I'd ever known. Me, who suffered through so many miscarriages I'd stopped counting.

Before the accident, I guess maybe I felt like I'd struggled enough in life, that in some ways God owed me. I never had a reason before Ethan's death to question God's goodness, but I found myself grappling with questions I had never asked before: Is He really good? Does God actually "take care" of His people? Does He really love me? Why was I chosen to bear this burden? Why is Anson now an only child? We tried so hard to make sure he wouldn't be an only child.

I also struggled with the accident not being Ethan's fault. I wanted to have a better, different, or easier explanation of what happened. Eventually, I had to admit to myself that the accident was his fault–but that still didn't give me an answer to my most-asked question–why?

Asking why and struggling through the hard and sometimes unanswerable questions has been, on the one hand, an exercise in futility, and on the other, a deepening in my faith and trust in a God I cannot understand this side of heaven.

Though I've never been given a satisfying answer by God or man, the struggle itself has made me long for heaven even more than I used to. I'd love to see the whole picture from God's point of view. It would help my grieving heart to see how the death of my son fits perfectly into God's loving, redemptive plan. Though I trust Him, the why will never make sense with mortal eyes, but I have found peace by believing in God's plan even when it doesn't make complete sense.

I know I'm not unique in my obsession with the why, and I don't think God is threatened by my questions. But in my questions and my struggles, I've found His friendship all the sweeter.

CHAPTER SEVEN

Grieve Together

From the first moment, our community swooped in and offered support, but most of the time, they would pull me in one direction and Chad in the other. I was so angry with Chad because I was blaming him for having guns in the house, so I didn't mind.

I hate to admit this, but the ladies were so good to me for a long time. Chad also had a great group of guys who were there for him, including our neighbor who had been with Chad at the time of the accident. We were showered with some of the sweetest gifts from Ethan's friends and our friends. Someone was constantly here with me, even just to sit with me. We would receive stacks of cards in the mail daily. We quickly started the Ethan Robbins Fund and people helped with fundraising. Men and women are just wired differently and being with our friends helped us process individually in the best way possible.

But the problem with grieving separately with our own friend groups was that I had and still have a hard time letting Chad see me grieve. Maybe if we had learned to grieve together in the early days it would be different, maybe it wouldn't. It was so very hard. I felt like if I talked about it, he felt to blame, and if I cried, he would feel bad and guilty also. He didn't deserve any more guilt than he already had, and I felt like he needed to know that no matter what God put us together and we would find a way to make it through.

For the first two years, we both cried almost daily, and we both hid our tears, and honestly, I still do it, and I know Chad does too. I wish we had never been pulled apart and had leaned on each other more. I know we will make it, but those first two years might have been easier had we learned to grieve together.

Again, I understand that we are not unique in this. I don't know why, but many people felt like they needed to mention to us the statistics on divorce after losing a child. So many people mentioned it, in fact, that I went and looked it up. Thankfully, the statistic wasn't as bad as I thought, but it doesn't matter anyway because I'm not going to live my life by statistics.

Three years into our grief, I realize that when tragedy strikes, as a married couple you need to pray together and invite the Holy Spirit to intervene. Sadly, Chad and I didn't know how to do this. Of course, we knew how to pray, but about this subject, we just didn't have words. I know that our pastors and some of our friends prayed with us, but I wish someone had the conversation with us about talking through everything and making space to grieve together.

However, even as I write this, I think this part of our story isn't over. We will likely struggle with this grief for the rest of our lives, and there is room to grow and open communication lines.

CHAPTER EIGHT

Forgive

I have noticed many things along this journey and one of them is that most people who have lost a child blame someone or something. Even years down the road, they still harbor unforgiveness. Ironically, I never seemed to realize this until I started talking to other parents who have lost children.

After I lost Ethan, I began to notice the tendency people have to blame others in their loss. I saw it in myself as well. I was struggling to forgive. I knew I had to forgive, but sometimes the feelings of blame, anger, and unforgiveness would creep back in. Forgiving myself and Ethan has been hard.

Early on I was angry with Chad, wanting to blame him. I knew better than to blame him, but I felt like I needed to hear him say he was sorry. Ethan was Chad's best friend, my brain knew he would have never done anything to allow him to get hurt, but my heart needed an answer to why.

I believed Chad hadn't properly cleared the gun a few weeks prior when he saw a snapping turtle at the pond. I know this sounds mean, but they kill all of our ducks so Chad tried to lessen their population when he could. But Chad said he and Ethan had only shot the gun a few times at a firing range. We don't know how there was one still in the chamber, but there was.

Chad and I were rarely alone with all the people in and out the weeks after Ethan died. My frustration grew and I began to blame Chad. It came to a head and one day my pent-up anger exploded, "Are you ever going to tell me you are sorry?" I confronted Chad with all my anger and sorrow. In his own anger and sorrow he got angry and stormed out.

I was so angry and prayed for wisdom. I poured my heart out and asked God why didn't we do this or that and I felt that same quiet voice say, you couldn't have changed it, it was just his day. I heard this so many times, but it was so hard to believe.

Eventually, Chad did say he was sorry. As soon as he said it, I knew he had nothing to be sorry about. The accident wasn't Chad's fault. He and Ethan were so close, Chad would never have done anything to have caused him harm. With Chad off the hook, I was left trying to forgive myself and Ethan.

Ethan's death was accidental, but he did cause it. A parent's number one job is to keep their child alive, and I failed at this with Ethan. I have begged God to tell Ethan I am sorry for not preventing the accident. An eternal perspective however looks through the lens that our death date is determined before birth and even the most dedicated parent has no control. I had to move past blaming myself for Ethan's accident. I knew if I didn't, I would be stuck and never move forward in a healthy way.

CHAPTER NINE

Remember Them Well

I couldn't throw away anything of Ethan's. It was easier for me to give some of his things away to his friends, but throwing anything of his away was too hard. We went through everything and made piles of t-shirts and sweatshirts that we would keep. Chad and Ethan wore the same size and if it was something that Chad wanted, we kept it. We had another pile of T-shirts that we would turn into two quilts, which was a great way to keep and use them.

Ethan's signature look was tobacco-colored pants and shorts from American Eagle. We made piles of them as well. All of them got sent to a talented seamstress who made teddy bears out of them. She made so many bears! Each one had a little heart on the left side and a red ribbon tied in a bow around the neck. We tried to give one to most of Ethan's friends. This was money well spent! It was good to connect in grief over Ethan with a little piece of his "signature look."

There were other items, like Ethan's most-worn dress shirts, that we weren't ready to turn into anything. We weren't ready for them to get cut into pieces. One of Ethan's blue dress shirts did recently get turned into a teddy bear with khaki pants made from Ethan's pants. I feel like we are finally making progress.

Surely, we could part with socks and underwear? Surely, we could not. But, for now, we're okay with that. We put his shoes and clothes into totes in his old closet.

We also left some things out: his favorite shoes. They were at the bottom of the stairs before he died, and they sat there so long they accumulated cobwebs. When I finally decided to move them, I decided to put them upstairs in the corner of the room he died in. It was his hang-out room and he always slept up there in the spare bed, so leaving his shoes in there felt appropriate.

I didn't intend for Ethan's room to become a shrine, but it kind of just happened. So many people gave us so many wonderful gifts and items to remember Ethan. It was nice to have a place to keep them all. My dear friend made a shadow box of Ethan's football things which brought me comfort. We decided to make one similar for Anson, so it balanced out. They had won the championship when Anson was a senior and Ethan was a freshman, so the seniors got to keep their jerseys.

Chad has kept Ethan's Tahoe in perfect condition. We couldn't sell it. Chad keeps it shining like a new penny and drives it just enough to make sure it stays in good working order. I have to admit when I see it drive off or back up the driveway, my heart sinks. Ethan should be behind that wheel. Even though he isn't, we will most likely keep his car for the rest of our lives.

Ethan's room is now a family room again. There are a lot of photos of Ethan simply because we have been given so many, but I won't be surprised if Ethan's wall space shares space with Anson and Caitlyn and the family they will one day have.

It seems as though we all need to remember our loved ones in our own ways, whether it all gets boxed up and stored, thrown out, donated, or kept exactly where it was. It's different for everyone.

In addition to remembering him with his things, we added other ways of remembering him, too. We decided to get a Witherspoon Rose Culture Memory Rose Garden planted right in front of our house in honor of Ethan. The gorgeous visual beauty of the roses is a constant reminder of the beautiful life of my son.

The expense was worth every penny. I was thankful for a beautiful reminder of Ethan that we and anyone who passes our home can see. Since it is extremely difficult for me to visit Ethan's grave site, I am thankful to have a place like this to remember him.

Even in the years after Ethan was gone, friends still give us gifts to remind us and remember him. It helps to know that others have not forgotten.

PART 3

In Grief, Keep The Faith

I believe in God the Father, who holds the world in the palm of His hand yet can list the name of every person on earth who's ever lived. I believe in Jesus Christ, His only Son, in whom every single cell and atom holds together and who calms storms with a word. I believe in the work of the Holy Spirit, endlessly comforting, perfectly guiding, and consistently helping. And I believe in the goodness of my God, despite my lack of understanding, despite the storm, despite this grief that lurks inside me like unexploded ordnance.

I do have hope. Despite every attempt to destroy it, and if I don't behave differently–in grief as in joy–what's the point of all these beliefs?

CHAPTER TEN

Never Forsaken

I would have never made it forward on this path if it wasn't for Jesus. However, in my darkest, deepest struggle, I realized I felt forsaken by God because of the accident. He had always taken care of me and our family, and Ethan's accident felt like God had rejected me.

In Deuteronomy 31 it says, *"He will be with you, He will not leave you nor forsake you; do not fear nor be dismayed,"* but was that promise for me as well as Israel? There were more places in scripture that gave my head the assurance, but my heart needed assurance too that I wasn't forsaken by God. I had to do a deep dive into the word and concept "forsaken" and how it related to me and God.

The Greek word for "forsaken" is egkataleipo (pronounced eng-kat-al-i'-po) meaning to abandon, desert, leave in straits, leave helpless. Now I was starting to get it. This was exactly how I was feeling. Grief left me in the desert. The word abandon resonated. I knew God was with me, but I felt I had lost His favor on that dreaded day in May of 2021.

Through my study I realized how immensely thankful I am that Jesus sent us a helper when He left this world. The Holy Spirit has been with me through it all, in the saddest and darkest times. I'm not alone now; I wasn't alone when Ethan died, and I won't be alone in the future. I can't imagine what it would be like to live without the Holy Spirit.

John 14:15-17 in The Message version has encouraged me, "*I will talk to the Father, and he'll provide you another Friend so that you will always have someone with you. This Friend is the Spirit of Truth. The godless world can't take him in because it doesn't have eyes to see him, doesn't know what to look for. But you know him already because he has been staying with you and will even be in you!*"

This verse was for me! Knowing in my heart and my head that the Holy Spirit was present with me at all times gave me the "peace that passes all understanding" described in Philippians 4:7.

That peace didn't mean my sadness went away, but I knew we had been given this peace to get through the visitation and funeral and to be able to continue on in this journey not forsaken. And though the days have been dark, I have never felt as close to God as I have these last three years. These are the days that He has made His presence known and holds us so close.

CHAPTER ELEVEN

Find Community

Before losing Ethan, we had a Life Group of about thirty people who would meet in our home every Friday night. We would eat together, pray together, and just fellowship. After losing Ethan our community has only expanded, and I am so grateful for that. They have supported us, loved us so well, and met our practical needs in so many ways. I also appreciated how Ethan's community supported us.

Ethan was a rising senior so there were so many senior activities and I think we were invited to every single one. We went to some, and they were very hard. It feels like the ones we said yes to were terribly hard, and the ones we said no to, we ended up wishing we had said yes to.

We went to senior night, and during halftime, at the football game he should have been playing at, they included us and gave me a rose, just like all of the other moms. Chad and I were both in tears. I will never forget wearing our Choose Joy T-shirts and Chad wearing Ethan's cowboy hat.

I always worried that our being there may have stolen some of Ethan's classmates' and teachers' joy, but they were all so kind and gracious to us. We were so blessed to be part of such an amazing school.

Another community we now belong to is the community of parents who have lost children. It's a club you never wanted to be a part of, where you are kindred spirits within moments of meeting. Those were some of the first people we wanted to talk to after Ethan's death, and now, we try to reach out whenever we hear of some new family that has joined our community.

Parents who have lost a child understand each other in ways that most others cannot. I wouldn't be where I am today if I didn't have others to lean on when the waves of grief start raging.

CHAPTER TWELVE

Stay In The Word

Just a few months after losing Ethan I became obsessed with heaven. My son was there, I wanted to be there now more than ever, and I was hungry to learn everything I could about heaven. I asked many people, drilling them about what they knew about heaven. I daydreamed about heaven and what Ethan was doing there. I begged Jesus to come get me and save me from my agony. I wanted to understand a piece of Ethan's current whereabouts. A friend knew this and invited me to take a Bible class at a local Bible College.

In the end, the class was about Genesis, so I didn't learn that much about heaven, but what I learned was so encouraging to my faith during this difficult time. I knew staying in God's word would help me stay grounded through grief, but I had a hard time concentrating while reading. Whereas before I had led Bible studies and daily been in the word and in prayer, now I was having a hard time even reading my Bible. I just wasn't sure how I would get through. It felt like none of the promises were for me and reading any type of rebuke was so difficult to read.

I found a creative solution! I bought a Bible that had a lot of words and images to color. I was able to think slowly through the scripture as I colored the pictures. It brought me a lot of peace, and I was happy to learn spending time in scripture didn't look just one way. I could still be in God's word even if I was having trouble reading it like I used to.

I had to lean on God and allow Him to continue to heal my broken heart, even though healing from this tragedy felt impossible.

The psalmist makes an audacious claim about God, *"He heals the brokenhearted and binds up their wounds" (Psalm 147:3).* This verse was one I clung to tightly in my darkest days. It captures the profound truth that God is not only aware of my pain but is also actively involved in the healing process for those who trust in Him.

During this time of heartbreak, tragedy, and great loss, I had to relearn what it meant to lean on God. I had to rely on Him for things even as simple as my next breath. Human abilities didn't cut it, but God's ability to heal my broken heart is real.

Healing is a journey I'm still on. It is a series of stages where God slowly restores me and comforts me–the brokenhearted–that He promises in this verse.

This reliance has made my relationship with God more intimate, fully relying on the Great Physician who heals and gently binds up my wounds. I have had to learn how to trust God way more than I ever had. Healing requires trust because, after tragedy, God doesn't seem to be very trustworthy. I had to rediscover His trustworthiness in the midst of tragedy. I had to invite Him to enter into all of the places of my heart, especially the most fragile and broken places. I had to acknowledge that He, and only He, has the power to bring wholeness to these broken places.

This act of surrender is not a sign of weakness but a sign of strength. Strength that comes only from trusting the only One who knows the end from the beginning and has the ability to make beauty from ashes.

I want to share with you some of my favorite "Lifeline Verses."

Exodus 14:14, "The LORD will fight for you; you need only to be still." You might think this isn't the best Lifeline Verse for someone

grieving but consider the person who feels someone is at fault for their loved one's death. They are definitely ready to fight, but they don't have to. Their Father in heaven will fight for them.

This verse is one that you can grab ahold of when you can barely catch your next breath: *Psalm 34:18 (NIV), "The LORD is close to the brokenhearted and saves those who are crushed in spirit."*

2nd Corinthians 4:8-9 (NKJV) says, *"We are hard-pressed on every side, yet not crushed; we are perplexed, but not in despair; persecuted, but not forsaken; struck down, but not destroyed."* If you find yourself feeling forsaken like I did, grab ahold of this Lifeline Verse and tell yourself you are not forsaken; you might be struck down, but you are not destroyed. Our minds have a way of believing what we tell them.

When we go through trauma, we can often end up with some irrational fears. I know I certainly did, and I am still working through them. I had so much fear when I knew Anson and Caitlyn were driving to and from Florida for their honeymoon. Maybe you are experiencing something similar? God's word is clear that He doesn't want us to fear, but if you need this reminder, this is an excellent Lifeline verse.

2nd Timothy 1:7, "For God has not given us a spirit of fear, but of power and of love and of a sound mind."

Matthew 11:28-30 (NKJV), "Come to Me, all you who labor and are heavy laden, and I will give you rest. Take My yoke upon you and learn from Me, for I am gentle and lowly in heart, and you will find rest for your souls. For My yoke is easy and My burden is light."

The burden of grief can be so heavy, but Jesus has offered to take that burden from us. When a wave of grief is crashing over you and you can't seem to steady your feet, remember this truth.

CHAPTER THIRTEEN

Continue To Worship

Before Ethan passed away, I was in a good place spiritually. I was leading an online Bible study every weekday which I started during Covid-19. I kept a prayer journal and loved praying for people day after day. I loved seeing and recording answered prayers. And I also went to church as often as I could during the pandemic. Thankfully, this routine continued after Ethan's death.

Even though the consistent routine of going to church on Sundays was extremely difficult and I cried every week, it was good for me to get out, to see people who loved me and cared about our family, and to worship God as a corporate body. Sitting through church was so hard for so long. Something–anything–would set me off, and I would cry for the entire service. It still happens. I think if I had gotten out of the routine of going to church after Ethan's death, I would have never had the courage to go back. I'm so grateful church is a safe place for me to be real.

I noticed I believed so many messages of condemnation. I consistently felt like a complete failure, and I often wondered if I hadn't done enough or said the right thing to be covered by God's love and favor.

I saw the example in the Bible of Job, "a blameless and upright man, who fears God and shuns evil," and had to grapple with Job's suffering and my own. Job was a really good man, yet he was specifically selected for a terrible amount of suffering. It was the first time I could see how Jesus bridges the gap between my effort and my failure. I can never do enough good things to be worthy of redemption. But instead, I'm worthy of redemption not because of what I've done, but because of what Jesus did.

Being a good person doesn't secure my salvation or a stress-free, tragedy-free life. Knowing Jesus doesn't ensure a stress-free or tragedy-free life. But, knowing Jesus lets me live a life free from condemnation. My grief and my faith can coexist. I can choose joy while I'm weeping.

CHAPTER FOURTEEN

Write

I find comfort in writing; I always have. But after Ethan passed away, for a short while, I just couldn't hold a pen and write much beyond, "We love you and miss you and will see you again." I began sharing some of my words on a Facebook group called Remembering Ethan Robbins created early on for friends and family members to share memories and photos with us. It became an outlet that helped us so much. It was so encouraging to get the support and kind feedback from the members of that group.

I struggled with the finality of losing Ethan. I hated knowing I'd never speak to him again. Writing, for me, smoothed the sharp edge of this reality. I often write as if I am writing to Ethan. We know he isn't reading what we are writing, but writing to him, even for pretend, helps heal my broken heart just a little bit.

Some days were difficult and words did not come easy, but my writer's block didn't last long. I wrote many things to purposely remember who Ethan was. I wrote about him sometimes daily, some posted online, and sometimes not. The posts acted as a wonderful, interactive grief journal. I loved that we could post photos and that group members could post theirs. There were so many photos I had never seen of Ethan. I drew much encouragement and strength from the support our friends and family expressed.

Though I know the grief space is a lonely place, we've been blessed to have so many people stay present with us. By writing regularly, people were able to observe and interact with our grief in a unique way that left us feeling encouraged, not depressed.

Grief changes people. I really didn't want grief to change me, and I fought it pretty hard in the beginning, but eventually I learned to embrace it. I am not the same person I was, and that is okay.

Grief doesn't have to be as public. I could have easily written to Ethan privately in a journal or on my computer, but I was so encouraged by the community that formed from processing my grief out loud.

CHAPTER FIFTEEN

Find A Focus

Not long after we lost Ethan, the children's director left our church campus, and I was asked to take over. I needed something to focus on, so I said yes. It has proved to be so healing. Every time a sweet child runs to me to give me a hug, I just melt. They will never know how much they have helped me heal, but hopefully, someday they find out.

When we help other people, it activates the reward center in our brains and releases serotonin, dopamine, and endorphins. We feel better after volunteering because it is really good for us. Trauma can cause us to have very low levels of these hormones. I am convinced volunteering after loss is a must for our mental health.

Just a day or so after losing Ethan, I got a text from someone who said we would need to find purpose for our pain or it would overtake us. She explained how they did a spaghetti supper, a silent auction, and a golf tournament to raise money for the memorial scholarship in her child's honor.

This suggestion sparked a purpose for Chad and me because we had been wanting to do something. We felt helpless and wanted our son to be remembered in a tangible way, so we had T-shirts made. Thankfully, Chad's sister is a talented graphic designer who quickly created the perfect design. A friend from church designed a website and handed it over to Chad to manage. We were delighted to sell so many shirts! People were so generous in their support of our cause. During a time of helplessness, it felt good to have a purpose.

Very early on, within a matter of hours, generous people gave to our church so that we could begin a scholarship fund for private Christian schooling in Ethan's honor. We started slowly, just simply by asking for donations instead of flowers at the funeral.

We were so blessed to get several very large donations that helped us clear up a few accounts for families who could use the financial blessing.

We weren't really sure what it would look like, but we quickly named it the Ethan Robbins Fund. Its goal would be to help students deepen their relationship with Jesus by helping ease the financial burden of Christian school. We would focus on the life that Ethan lived. From the beginning we worked with The Ethan Robbins Fund as our job. It has brought purpose to our pain. It keeps me busy and just the thought of helping kids have a Christian school experience like my boys did makes me feel so good.

We raised enough money in the very early months to create an endowment but decided, after seeking advice from trusted friends, that we wanted to spend the money as it was raised. One friend in particular reminded us of the Parable of the Talents, so every year we have given scholarships as the money has come in.

At this point I still couldn't go to the grocery store. And Chad and I could hardly look at each other when we were alone. How in the world were we going to be able to fundraise as we were still in the thick of our grief? Would we ever get comfortable telling people "what happened," and would people see it as something worthy of support?

Fundraising can be very time consuming and that is so good for someone grieving. If you can get your focus on something other than your grief for at least a few hours a day it can be a blessing. I find that when we aren't busy promoting the next event we tend to get sad.

Also, I've learned I need to prepare for the grief waves when an event finishes. I can be so busy during fundraising season that when it comes to a halt, I'm hit by the wave. I am so thankful to have friends who know this is going to happen to me and stick close by when it is all over.

Thankfully our years of Direct Selling had provided a residual income for us so that we could focus on healing and not having the stress of work. We still "worked," but we were able to pay people to take most of the burden from us. Because of that, Chad and I were able to do something both fun and unexpected together.

In the fall after Ethan passed away we purchased two homes and renovated both of them. It was very involved and used so much creativity. Like fundraising, we also treated the renovations like a job. Every morning we'd wake up and go to work. We demoed two bathrooms and a kitchen. We had some help but did everything we possibly could ourselves. It was great therapy. Anson moved into one of them before he and his wife got married, and she had a beautiful home to move into after the wedding!

CHAPTER SIXTEEN

Fight Back

I didn't want it to, but grief has changed me. My personality, my energy levels, and even what I enjoy doing on a Saturday night are different now. And that's okay. But I am committed to the fight to choose joy, just as I'm committed to be better instead of bitter. And it is a fight, no two ways about it.

Because of our deep grief, the enemy saw this as a great time to attack, and for a while, I was defenseless to his lies. One of the dark, enemy-fueled thoughts I entertained early on was that Chad should leave me. He was only 43; he could find a younger, much more beautiful wife and start over. I felt old, like I would never be fun again, and I was too old to have more children.

After losing Ethan and knowing that Anson was now an only child, I wanted another child. I was heartbroken. I didn't push to have more kids when the boys were young, and I was sad at 45 I wouldn't have any more babies. At the time, it made sense to me that Chad could do better, start a new life with a new wife and new kids, and move on from me.

These irrational thoughts took over one night and I packed up the dogs and left the house. I drove around for a couple of hours.

Chad called and called and begged me to come home, and I finally did. Returning that night was the beginning for me of fighting back.

I had to build up a defense against the lies of the enemy, and I chose 2 Corinthians 10:5 as my standard. "Demolish arguments and every pretension that sets itself up against the knowledge of God, and take captive every thought to make it obedient to Christ."

I began to practice taking each dark thought captive to gain control over what and how I was thinking about myself and my life. It was something I had to learn and repeat, almost like muscle memory, in order not to let my thoughts and actions spin wildly out of control.

I memorized that verse and repeat it to this day whenever the enemy tries to tempt my mind and thoughts toward how Ethan died. Those thoughts have the power to cripple me, and I can lose days of productivity if I allow my mind to go there for too long.

Examining each thought and evaluating it against the backdrop of scripture is a skill I continue to work on and use in my daily life, and I have noticed the habit has enhanced my spiritual life by helping me fight back against the schemes of the enemy.

CHAPTER SEVENTEEN

Choose Joy

As I mentioned earlier, Ethan's life verse is one I have kept in the forefront of my mind. It reminds me over and over to CHOOSE JOY. I want to choose joy so badly, but I keep falling short. Thankfully, I feel like God has given me permission to just grieve in order to get through every season. I have learned that choosing joy doesn't mean being happy every day, all day, but that grief and joy co-mingle.

Biblical joy is so much more than feeling happy. Happiness is dependent on our circumstances which change constantly. Joy comes from a relationship with Jesus and knowing that His helper, the Holy Spirit, is a constant companion and comfort in times of need. Jesus is the true source of joy and peace despite the circumstances.

We miss Ethan every day. That will never change, but we know we will see him again. Our grief will be something we carry until our last breath, but we have discovered we can choose joy even while we miss Ethan. We can enjoy life's richest blessings while simultaneously experiencing the ache of grief.

Maybe you won't understand the calling I felt even from the beginning, this burden to Choose Joy, but from very early on when

I began catching my first glimpses of life beyond the fog, I knew that if I grieved like everyone else, I would not be living what I believed to be true.

And what I believe to be true is that because of Jesus' great sacrifice, we are confident we will be reunited with Ethan again in heaven. This journey is not one I would pick or wish on anyone. However, I have found joy and peace in the darkest places because that's where I found God.

PART 4

In Grief, Be Practical

When Ethan died people stepped up. Most of the time it was kind, helpful, and needed. Friends brought us meals and came over to sit, listen, and cry with us. They helped us clean up, move boxes, and sort through Ethan's things. Neighbors did our yard work. We were sent flowers and cards and had a meal train for months. I was given a huge stack of books, but I still haven't made it through.

However, it wasn't all helpful. There were uncomfortable moments that added to our grief. Some people, though I'm sure well-meaning, made judgemental, nosy, or unhelpful comments. We were gossiped about and questioned. The criticism felt extra hard and hurtful.

I have learned a lot about grief and grieving, and though I still have a long way to go, these are some practical steps that have helped me

Social Re-Entry

I remember a trip to Hobby Lobby that first fall. I had decided to do a memory tree for Ethan, and I needed to get some ribbon. I had already gone to Hobby Lobby earlier that week with Chad, and he always makes any trip ok. He can just wave and say "hey" real quick and move on. I just can't do that, so I get stuck talking to people and there it is again, and it is almost like another funeral. The "what happened?" question is still really, really hard for me.

So, I figured I could go to Hobby Lobby and grab some ribbon and get home just fine. Well, that is the farthest thing from what happened. First of all, I saw a distant relative of Chad's, and they were so sweet, but I just didn't need to hear the normal "I am so sorry" spiel; I just needed to get in and out.

We were heading into our first holiday season after losing Ethan and I was still very fragile. I managed to make it through that conversation and in the ribbon aisle and then I bumped into someone who didn't know that Ethan had passed away. She asked how the boys were and how old they are now, and I fell apart. Then she asked the dreaded "what happened?" I grabbed a bunch of ribbon that I didn't even like because I had to get out of there. As soon as I got in my car alone I screamed and cried all the way home.

These awkward and uncomfortable social situations lasted for a long time, and it took a long time to not feel devastated after each one. I learned that it was okay to say no if I didn't feel up to it. Sometimes I got Chad to go with me, but it didn't always work out. I would have to consider every situation, sometimes choosing to go and sometimes choosing not to. I could have told him I was scared to go alone, and I bet he would have dropped everything and gone with me.

I probably should have forced myself to the grocery store more, to get out in public more, but Chad didn't ever seem to have a hard time going places, so he always had us covered. It was just really hard to see people sometimes. I knew that one day I would have to get better about this, but for quite a while I chose to say no to the grocery store and most anywhere I might see people I hadn't yet seen. Now I can go to the grocery store alone. This sounds silly if you've never lost a child or been through major trauma, but those of you who know, I know you get it. Being alone in public can be so hard.

To this day, that ugly ribbon from Hobby Lobby that I grabbed in such a hurry is still on Ethan's memory tree. Because when I see that ribbon I remember how fragile I once was. It is a little reminder of how far I have come on my grief journey.

Buy the Soft Tissues

This might sound silly, but it is so true: splurge on the soft tissues for yourself and friends who are grieving.

Keep a box of tissues in every room. Grief comes in waves and at the most random times. The tissue supply should be abundant everywhere for a long time because there is nothing more gross than having to clean up your latest grief wave by wiping snot all over your favorite sweatshirt.

I am comforted when I see a tissue box nearby at church or a friend's home. It kind of feels like an open invitation to cry and grieve. The tissue box has become my symbol of permission to "let it all out."

Let It Out

There is something very powerful about screaming. For some of you, it might need to be directed into a pillow. Maybe you have neighbors or children that would be scared by the noise. Or if you live far away from people, you can simply go outside. Maybe a walk through the woods. Now I am not promising you that someone might not hear you and try to come to your rescue, but the release will be worth it either way.

I did my fair share of crying into my pillow so Chad wouldn't hear me. And my most favorite place to scream was when driving in my car. There was something about driving alone that was so tough. I had been used to putting on music whenever I was in the car, but music was such a huge part of who Ethan was that listening to songs was too tough.

Usually, I would try to make sure I had someone to talk to until I got to my destination, or I would listen to an interesting podcast, but sometimes I just screamed and cried as I drove along.

An Object of Comfort

I was surprised to find a lot of comfort, especially in the early days of grief, from a soft, cuddly teddy bear. A kind friend gave it to me and because it had a place for a photo, I hugged it and Ethan's picture close to my heart.

It seemed childish, but it made me feel better. If you need another reason beyond that, there is scientific evidence that cuddling something soft and comforting greatly lowers your levels of the stress hormone cortisol. Oxytocin, a hormone that relaxes and soothes the mind, is also released when you cuddle, even with a stuffed animal.

This bear has traveled everywhere we have been, and I am not even ashamed to admit it. Get yourself a soft teddy bear; you'll be glad you did.

Find A Lifeline Verse

"May the God of Hope fill you with all JOY and peace as you trust in Him, so that you may overflow with Hope by the power of the Holy Spirit." Romans 15:13

This verse was written by the Apostle Paul about 50 years after Jesus died. It was a prayer for the Christians in Rome, and it is often used in churches today as a closing benediction. It is a powerful statement about what God can do in the heart and mind of every Christian. Paul makes this request of the God of hope, another beautiful name for God.

This verse became incredibly special to us because it's the one Ethan chose for his life verse in 10th grade. It has become our "lifeline verse." I don't know why, but I started googling and noticed that a lot of people had shortened the verse to "Choose Joy." I decided to run with that, and it is now what gets us through the tough days.

The God of hope can certainly help us to Choose Joy in every situation because joy is not circumstantial, happiness is. So, no matter how sad we are, or what kind of grief wave has mercilessly crashed into us, we can be assured of Biblical Joy because Biblical Joy is found only through a relationship with Jesus.

I pray you find a verse of your own to help get you through the hard days. Memorize it, study it, and find out what the writer was going through at the time that verse was written. Repeat it often.

It's Okay To Say "No"

So many times, we need people to come in and take charge and just get things done. I know I needed a whole village to help me. There will be so many times that you can say yes to the people who love and care about you and want to help, but right now, let's focus on some things that it is okay to say no to.

This one is going to be the most simple and it almost feels silly to write it. Now, keep in mind that we live in Eastern North Carolina, and we Southerners really like to feed people. No matter the occasion, we are going to make a "spread." A spread simply means any food we think our family likes; we will just cook that, all of that. And add a little extra butter to it and serve it up on our finest Sunday best china. We just love to feed people. So naturally, whenever there is a death in the community, the food starts coming through the door. Did I mention the fried chicken and Eastern NC BBQ? You will have lots of that!

So, the food comes in the door, and as wonderful as that is, you don't have time, energy, or the wherewithal to even go through a drive thru for your family. But you can't even catch your breath long enough to swallow water, let alone heavy comfort food. You just can't breathe.

I remember people telling me to eat in those first few days and I just kept saying no. Finally, someone was so relentless that I took a bite of chicken salad, and I am sure it was delicious because I know who made it and she makes the best! But as I took that first bite, someone walked in the door that I knew was hurting so much and our grief just collided, and I couldn't breathe. I was now choking on that tiny morsel of food. I just knew I wasn't ready yet.

I still get like this sometimes. There are certain friends of Ethan's that I can just feel their grief. They loved him, too. I am guilty of not fully understanding that someone else is hurting because he is gone besides just me. Especially Chad. He is so strong I sometimes forget that his heart is broken too.

I had tried so hard to convince people that I am a stress eater and if I did lose a few pounds over the next little time frame, I would most certainly find it. Maybe if someone is so thin that they can't even lose one pound, feel free to force-feed them, but otherwise if they say no, just let them fast for a little bit. In the Bible, when people grieved they would often fast also. So, allow yourself or your loved ones to fast for a little bit if they need to. Eventually they will eat; just give them time.

I also want you to know that it is okay to say no to anything that doesn't bring you joy, especially in the beginning. If you don't want to leave your home for days on end, that is ok. Just remember that the longer you stay away from things like work and church, the harder it can be to go back.

I personally didn't stop going to church because that has always been a safe place for me, with the exception of my hiding in an unused classroom before the worship team went up. I was trying so hard to hold it together and if someone made me sad by saying something very well-meaning, I would just lose it. Singing and crying are quite hard to do at the same time and it was just better to keep myself tear-free as long as I could. There are always times during worship when the Holy Spirit grabs you, and you cry anyway.

Don't Go Alone

In situations like this you should have a friend that truly "gets you" close by. This friend needs to be savvy enough to know how to read the room for you. Maybe you choose a word or phrase to use so they know you need their help to divert someone and give you a break.

Even the most well-meaning person at times could leave me in tears and I needed help to avoid or get out of the conversation. A trusted friend can do this. I didn't need someone all the time, but at certain events, it was important I had someone by my side. I found when I am alone, people will ask or say things that can upset me, but if there is someone with me their words don't hit quite as hard.

Don't Forget About The Kids Left Behind

I am so thankful someone took the time to give me this message early on. A child who had lost a sibling reached out to me to tell us to try hard not to forget the living. They felt that their parents had forgotten them and that they couldn't be happy anymore.

At first, I had to force myself to find normalcy for my living child. It was such an overwhelming loss that it was truly difficult to think about anyone else and how they were affected.

I have done a lot, I mean a lot a lot, of things wrong, but I think I handled remembering Ethan and celebrating Anson and Caitlyn at their wedding pretty well. I believe there is a fine line between honoring our lost loved ones and making our living loved ones feel unimportant. I try to be mindful about this although I am sure I miss the mark. Sometimes I do subtle things so that I know I am remembering Ethan but I don't make it uncomfortable for anyone else.

I don't know if we did everything just right with Anson, I am sure we didn't, but I am glad someone cared enough to tell us to try hard to remember those that we are still on this side of heaven.

Additionally, I hadn't even thought about Ethan's friends until recently. It finally hit me a few months ago that even though his friends don't post about him much anymore on social media, the trauma of losing a friend won't soon leave their minds. Maybe I should check in on them more instead of expecting them to check in on me.

Find Positive Distractions

In grief, I haven't done everything perfectly (there's no perfect way to grieve), but there is one thing I have learned to do well. I find it necessary to be able to take my thoughts captive very quickly. Dwelling on Ethan's death only sends me spiraling into a dark place where I can lose myself for days. To counter this, I have learned to paint, color, sew, and participate in several other hobbies.

Painting, crafting, and creating have helped me on my grief journey in more ways than just being distractions. I felt so good after painting one day that I did some research and discovered that just the act of creating art can reduce cortisol levels and activate dopamine and other feel-good chemicals that can boost your mood and relieve stress. I felt like I'd found an amazing natural antidepressant!

I don't love shopping, but I do enjoy buying small gifts–or better yet, making them–for friends and family. Two years ago, I dried fruit and packaged it in cute jars with paper and twine tops. This past Christmas, I painted oyster shells and transformed them into ornaments.

These are all what I call my positive distractions, but my favorite distraction has got to be puppies! During the boredom of 2020, Ethan asked if we could have puppies, so we brought a second dog home. He never got to see them, but the first litter of five puppies was born on his first birthday in heaven, January 28th.

We have had three litters now and they are so precious to us, a true gift from God. We're keeping one, Pecan, out of this last litter, but the rest of them have been sold to wonderful people with the profits going to the Ethan Robbins Fund.

It's possible but quite hard to be sad while you are holding a tiny puppy, and for me, they are a way of God showing us that He still loves us and cares about us as much as He ever has.

Be Aware Of Habits

In grief, many people turn to some type of coping mechanism. Some are good, some are harmful, but all coping mechanisms can turn harmful if they aren't lived in balance. I turned to food to cope. I still struggle with food addiction. I managed to pull myself together a little bit around the wedding and not eat quite as much. But when it was over, I started eating a lot again.

Even though I don't turn to food for comfort as much as I did right after Ethan died when I get sad, I find myself turning immediately to comfort food. I know better because it only makes me feel so bad, especially when my clothes won't fit!

I am glad I became aware of this addiction because I was able to recognize it and talk about it. There are many other habits people use to cope while in grief which can be extremely harmful if gone unchecked. In grief, I was tempted to hide my struggle with food because I felt ashamed. It was embarrassing. Though hard to treat, I was thankful it came to the surface so I could face it head on.

It's Okay To Celebrate

About a month after Ethan passed away, Anson and Caitlyn got engaged. Anson had asked Ethan for help planning the engagement and we think the idea was for them to go to Emerald Isle for the day and have Anson propose on the pier.

Now that Ethan was gone, Anson wanted help finding the perfect spot. I remember Chad and I didn't think we would have the energy to drive there and back in one day. Sleep was hard to come by at that point. We were still waking up to the sounds of each other crying in the middle of the night and waking up each morning in major shock that Ethan's death was real.

Anson was grieving, too. He was grieving hard. He had lost his only sibling. But he also wanted to move forward with his life with Caitlyn. We decided to go to Nags Head because it was the last place we had all been to the beach together as a family.

As I am sitting here writing this, it just seems surreal that we moved on so quickly to an engagement party and all of the wedding plans. I don't know how we did it. My emotions were all over the place, but I felt like if I could just help plan this wedding I could keep my mind occupied and could stay sane. I am pretty sure that I wasn't sane! I was so easily offended over the littlest things, and I'm quite certain I drove everyone crazy during that time.

Looking back, I can see I must have been terribly difficult to be around. I was like a spoiled child. You know the one that had something happen and then everyone just lets them have their way? That was me. I don't know how we got through all of the craziness, but somehow we did. I always wanted a daughter, and I am thankful I now have one.

It was hard to include Ethan in Anson and Caitlyn's wedding but yet not forget that it was Anson and Caitlyn's day, not Ethan's.

One of my favorite things we did to remember Ethan was a gorgeous memory table at Anson and Caitlyn's wedding, which Chad's sister helped me create.

We didn't go as far as to leave out the space Ethan would have stood or talk about him during the wedding. But Anson had a little tag with Ethan's photo on his lapel flower and I had someone paint a picture to look like Ethan was at the wedding.

Parades With Meaning

July 4th was probably Ethan's favorite holiday. He was always so patriotic. We started hosting a neighborhood cookout and fireworks very soon after we moved in. We eventually started doing a parade. Ethan just loved this. He was quiet and didn't like being the center of attention, but he was so proud to ride through the neighborhood with flags flowing.

That first July 4th was just brutal. I couldn't pull myself together to organize anything, but Ethan's best friend's mom, Leann, did. One of our neighbors even made posters that said We Miss You, Ethan. We rode in the parade, and I am pretty sure that I probably cried the whole time.

We haven't done the parade since, but I am thinking maybe this year we should! Maybe do a contest and really make it fun. I am pretty good at figuring out ways to generate money for Ethan's fund, and I think this could be a way!

Awkward Conversations

Year one, we didn't attend any Christmas parties. Seeing people for the first time since we lost Ethan was extremely difficult. Some people would stare and not speak a word; some would try and give their condolences, leaving me wondering what they really thought. And sometimes the worst would happen. Someone would ask those dreaded two words, "What happened?"

During the second Christmas season after losing Ethan, my best friend wanted Chad and I to go to our dear friend's Christmas party. I didn't think I was ready and told her so, but she said I would be okay, and joked she had a safe place for me in the corner.

I couldn't find anything to wear as it was unseasonably warm, so I threw on an old green and white striped, short-sleeved shirt and a cardigan with jeans and finally got there. We were instructed to hit up the glorious dessert table, and I did as I was told, with reluctance. I walked through the crowd, dying inside, and finally got to the dessert table.

As I went through the motions of collecting sweet treats on a tiny plate, I found myself standing next to the sweetest couple we used to go to church with. I tried to act normal and begin to chat and catch up with fear and trepidation. I spoke to the husband because he was closest to me. At first, he didn't recognize me, as I had gained some grief weight and had much blonder hair since he had seen me last.

He wisely didn't mention the weight, but he did mention my hair. I thought to myself, Ok, if we can just not go anywhere else with this conversation, I will be okay. But of course, as if on cue, the husband dove in, "So, how are your boys?" I pretended like I didn't hear him, but no luck. He asked again, "How are your boys?"

Starting to choke up but trying to hold it all together I said, "You know we lost Ethan last year, don't you?" He started to cry and was so apologetic. I couldn't hold the tears back anymore. The door was maybe four feet from me, and I was really scared I would cry so loud I would cause a huge scene.

I got to my car and stayed there for the rest of the evening. I did a lot of ugly, loud crying. Chad came and sat with me for a little bit.

We've just had our third Christmas without Ethan and I feel stronger than I did last year. I feel sad sometimes, but the grief has changed. This year, we attended two Christmas parties. At the first one, three different people asked me how many children I had and how old they were. I have learned that I can respond with a smile on my face and quickly say something like, "We have two boys, and one is in heaven now; how many children do you have?" Most of the time, they have a shocked look on their face, but start talking about their children and it isn't so awkward after all.

Holidays Are Hard

We've now celebrated our third Thanksgiving without Ethan, and the first one without Chad's mom. It was the first time I was excited about hosting since Ethan's passing, and I handled it well. Of course, I had visions of a perfect meal with no chaos, but that didn't happen. I had high hopes of everyone walking in at 5 p.m. ready to be served, but I was on the struggle bus trying to carve two turkeys when I didn't even know how to carve one! I sure missed having NaNa here (Chad's mom).

I was still a complete mess for the rest of the day, and I think a lot of it just had to do with timing. We had 21 people at our home and there should have been 23. Ethan and Chad's mom. I worked so hard all week to try to make this meal as similar to how it would have been with Chad's mom as possible. I guess Chad and I both were in survival mode, and we just had to figure out how to get through this day.

But that's a holiday! They're hard, no two ways about it. I remember that first Christmas after Ethan died–something that really helped me get through was getting a new tree, just for Ethan. I put Ethan's tree in the dining room. I bought ornaments representing things he loved and added several of the ornaments he made in preschool. Several friends gave us special ornaments for his tree.

Every year I add ornaments to the tree. I made oyster ornaments and I put his name on one and hung it on his tree. Several people have given me ornaments for his tree and it means a lot. I don't want to ever forget that he loved coffee and cinnamon rolls, the Grinch, and Cat in the Hat. This tradition helps me remember him at Christmas.

The first year I put Ethan's tree up way before Christmas, and I kept it up until spring. I put up both of Ethan's stockings, one on each fireplace. The second year, I only put up one. I don't know how long I will keep on putting his stocking up, but for now, it feels right.

As time has passed, I've slowly started to find myself again. I give myself a lot of grace which helps me not to be disappointed with myself when I don't have the energy to do the same things I did for previous Christmases. Some of the grace I show myself during the Christmas season is watching predictably sweet Hallmark movies and not making Christmas cookies. Baking up a storm in the kitchen was a season standard for me, but I haven't been able to pick that up again.

I still allow myself to let the waves of grief rush over me during the holidays. I don't know if the holidays will ever become easy or that Ethan's Birthday and death anniversary won't rock me to my core. But I can with every year they don't consume me for as long as they once did.

Holidays are hard. It is what it is.

Give Grace

When I first thought of writing this book, I wanted to call it Grieving Rules because that is, in part, how I have survived. I made rules for myself in the first year. I allowed myself to grieve all day, every day if needed, but I worked hard at the practice and discipline of taking my dark thoughts captive.

For year two, I modified my rules a bit, setting boundaries for myself because I felt like to keep allowing myself to grieve so deeply like this forever wasn't CHOOSING JOY; it was actually allowing my joy to be stolen.

I knew I was going to have days I could sit and eat ice cream and cry and days I was gonna try and be a little good to the world. In the first year, I grieved hard on Mondays. And the 17th of the month. Holidays and birthdays were so difficult. Even holidays I didn't like very much, such as Halloween, were devastatingly hard. I knew I wasn't ready to give up grieving holidays or birthdays — but Mondays. Maybe I could let Mondays go? So, I did!!

When I felt myself dreading Mondays in year two, I would stop myself in my tracks, say nope, and quickly take those thoughts captive! I sang a song in my head that made me feel at peace. I remembered Romans 15:13 and forced myself to choose joy and to think about the good memories.

For year two, Mondays would no longer control me. But I still allowed the 17th to wreck me if it needed to. I did a lot of writing on those days. I also did a lot of talking with other grievers. I wanted their best survival tips.

Now I'm in year three, and I've decided that I will only let holidays, birthdays, and May 17th devastate me. I'm not sure if I'll try and do anything differently in year four or not yet. But my point is this: let yourself grieve, but eventually set boundaries.

If your timeline is different from mine, if your grief rules are different, or if you think the idea of grief rules is silly–don't worry about it; just do what you must! But I will tell you like I was told: if you don't find purpose for your pain, you won't get better. I truly want us all to get better.

Afterword

A Word For Those Walking Beside Loved Ones In Deep Grief

Be Present and Listen

Lots of my friends would reassure me that if I ever needed to talk, I could call them. Well, sometimes I just needed them to listen to me say the same things over and over. It's not fair. Why us? Why me? Why, why, why?

If you are reading this from the perspective of trying to understand a friend or loved one, here is the number one thing they want. They want you to simply sit with them. Sometimes on the phone and sometimes in person. This is not always fun. They probably don't want to go out to eat and if they do, they will tell you and then do that.

Say Their Name

They want you to call or text them when a memory of their loved one pops up in your head or your Facebook memories. Send them the photos you come across of their loved one; it will likely be the highlight of their day. Don't be scared to say their loved one's name. They will appreciate you remembering them. One of the things we struggle with the most is the fear that our children and all of the good things they brought to this world will be forgotten. Help them make sure their loved one won't be forgotten; speak of them often.

Be Consistent

I had one friend who checked on me nightly for months. She didn't say how are you, she simply said, "Good night check." Every time she did this, I knew it was an open invitation to chat with her if I needed to. That made me feel so much better. I am so thankful for friends like her.

Try Not To Ask How They Are

The most complicated question I get asked is, "How are you?" and if I could, I would ban this question completely. Nearly three years later, the answer is still complicated. I will always be in grief. So even though I might be "good" because something positive happened, I'm simultaneously "not good" because I miss Ethan.

Instead of asking a grieving person, "How are you?" greet them with a comment or a compliment! You aren't insensitive for not asking how they are, you are respecting the complexity of the situation and greeting them in the moment. I know that "How are you?" is a well-meaning question, but it's a burden to answer.

If you are exceptionally close to the grieving person, if you are a part of their inner circle, it might be more acceptable to ask how they are doing, but even then, assume it's hard, they probably aren't doing great, and your presence is enough of an encouragement.

Conclusion

Early on I knew so little about the spirit of heaviness, basically prolonged grief. But I knew enough to know I couldn't stop living. I couldn't hole up in my closet and scream or become a recluse who never left the house.

I knew enough to know that if God left me here on this earth, He still had a good plan for me and things He wanted me to do. And I have tried to seek His face and discover what those things are.

And I've discovered what Christians for centuries have known to be true. Even in the unthinkable loss of a child, God is good. Contrary to the cliche, He will and often does give us more than we can bear–but He also keeps His promise to never leave us nor forsake us.

I am still very much in grief. In process. In change. But He is still very much by my side, through it all. And that is enough.

Acknowledgements

Chad, you have been my rock since 1996 when we met on that blind date. I know I am a lot to deal with and you have gracefully allowed me to pursue my dreams and even made my dreams your dreams and helped me achieve them.

Anson, I hope I never forget that you would come home from work in the early days and just sit with me. You were my safe space, and I could cry to you and didn't even have to talk. You just lent me your strong shoulder to cry on and that was so special.

Caitlyn, you are a trooper for putting up with all of our family's craziness. There is no doubt that you are the girl I prayed for, for so many years, to one day be Anson's wife. We thank God for you.

April and Charlie, thank you for dropping everything to come help us with anything needed. You two were such a great help in those early days and still today.

Brittany and Jon, thank you for sharing your precious children with us. Having them in our lives has been a huge blessing. Their hugs are the best medicine. Brittany, thank you for being the one to answer my call the night me, **Levi,** and **Elsie** ran away. I was so frantic I never even asked where you were. You graciously put up with me for at least an hour before I figured out you were at GWL!

Daphnee, I will never forget you showing up within minutes of finding out Ethan had passed away. You have become one of my dearest friends and I don't know what our family would do without you.

Jennifer, oh where do I begin? You always got the real me, and sometimes that was the very irrational me. Thank you for still trying to get me out of the house. I promise to go see that band you want me to go see very soon. Thank you for talking me into getting the rose garden; it has been a great source of therapy. I feel like you and **Jon** are always doing things for us and owe you BIG!

Shellie and Thomas, thank you for flying to NC to just be with us the second that the US border was open for Canadians to cross over. Your being here meant so much.

Taryn, thank you for the nightly check ins and so much more.

Tony, thank you for stopping everything to fly to NC for the funeral.

To **Ethan's friends** who visited us, sent flowers, text messages, and phone calls. Who showed up for the one-year memorial service by the pond, and keep showing up for us on the holidays that are so difficult. We see you and know you are hurting too.

Our Rise church family and especially our **Life Group.** God put you all in our lives for a reason and we just can't thank you enough for loving us. Thank you for helping us get the Ethan Robbins Fund going. There is no way we could have started it without you all.

To our work family. To the people who stepped in and helped lead our direct sales team. **The people at the gym** who were there for Anson when he needed someone to help complete a task or just a friend to chat with. **My Real Estate team**. You all stepped right in and made sure my phone didn't ring. You took on so many tasks for me for a very long time. Chad and I are both very grateful for each of you.

Faith Christian School. You have supported us from day one and we thank you. I could name so many teachers and staff right now because you are all wonderful. **Coach Jones** and **Mr. Harris** have unfortunately walked the same path that we have through the loss of their sons, **Ayden Jone**s and **Calvin Harris**. When you and so many others showed up and grieved with us around our kitchen table we knew that the school would be a source of comfort for us for years to come.

To **all our friends**, new and old, who began the child loss journey before us. Thank you for being there to sit with us in our grief and tell us the things that bring you comfort in hopes it would help us. For making us not feel so isolated. I wish I could name you all. You have helped us see that we can survive this grief as long as we keep our eyes on Jesus.

To **all of the volunteers** and **board members** of the Ethan Robbins Fund, thank you for always being ready to put in the work. And for forgiving me for doing four fundraisers in one week. I mean it sounded like a good idea until we were just out of steam at the end. You all worked so hard!

Everyone at Blue Hat Publishing but especially **Brandon, Jodi**, and **Rachael**. Brandon, you made me believe I could do this, and Jodi and Rachael, you exceeded every expectation I had about what this process should be like. What could have been very traumatic, you made joyful.

I could name **so many friends and family members** right now, but the list would be longer than the book! You know who you are, and I know you were here, and you will continue to be there for us, and us for you for the rest of our lives. I love you all.

And lastly, to **everyone who has purchased or donated to the Ethan Robbins Fund**, yes, even puppies! There were several large donors in the beginning, and without you, I don't know if the Ethan Robbins Fund would ever have gotten off the ground. We are so thankful for each of you. Thank you so very much.